Robots For News Sites

The Essential Guide To Success In Modern Journalism

I. O. FAITH

Copyright © 2024 I. O. Faith

All rights reserved. No part of this publication should be reproduced without the prior written permission from the author. This though, does not apply to a reviewer who might quote except for the purpose of highlight in his review.

ISBN: 9798322221555

DEDICATION

To Mark Hill, the programing guru I respect so much.

CONTENTS

	Acknowledgments	i
	Introduction	1
1	Define Your Objectives	3
2	Data Collection	5
3	Preprocessing	7
4	Model Selection	9
5	Training	13
6	Fine-tuning	15
7	Evaluation	17
8	Deployment	19
9	Testing And Optimization	21
10	Monitoring And Maintenance	23
11	Ethical Considerations	25
	Conclusion	27

ACKNOWLEDGMENTS

Thank you, Mark Hill for all the insights. Special thanks also goes to Rebecca Carton, the principal of Rainbow computer training.

INTRODUCTION

The world of journalism is moving at a very fast pace. Failure to keep pace will put you behind in the race. So, you must take advantage of new innovations that'll propel you forward. One such innovations is the use of bots in your news site. Yours is to train the bot and then relax. Your trained bot will handle the rest of the job in your behalf and better.

In this comprehensive guide, I'm going to show you all you need to know about using AI robot on your news sites. I will be talking to you about creating the bot, giving it a clear cut objective, gathering data to train the bot and standardizing it for consistency. I'm also going to teach you how to select your model, training and fine-tuning it.

Of course, I'm going to show you why and how to evaluate the output of your model. And you will finally learn to deploy it and integrate your trained model into your system. You will learn how to optimize your trained model through testing and fixes of issues that might be arising.

The final area I will teach you is maintenance and ethical factors that merit consideration.

At the end of this course you will be able to harness the

power of artificial intelligence to research, craft, and deliver timely and engaging headlines. You are going to watch and your trained bot will do all the job. You will enhance readers engagement, with your bot rolling out all the timely and relevant materials, gluing them to your news site.

Trust me, no other topic is more appropriate for our first chapter than fixing our objectives clearly in mind. So, in our very first chapter, we are going to define and understand the whole picture of our goal before ever proceeding to making the bot.

CHAPTER ONE
DEFINE YOUR OBJECTIVES

Defining objectives is the foundational step in creating an AI robot for generating news headlines. It involves meticulously outlining the entire scope, purpose, and parameters of the project to ensure its alignment with desired outcomes. Firstly, clarifying the scope entails identifying the specific areas or topics the AI robot will cover. This could range from global news, politics, finance, technology, entertainment, to niche areas like science or environmental affairs. Deciding on the breadth and depth of coverage is important for streamlining data collection and model training processes.

Secondly, determining the purpose involves understanding the intended function of the AI robot. Is it meant to inform, entertain, or both? Will it prioritize breaking news, in-depth analysis, or curated content? Defining the purpose helps in tailoring the model architecture, training strategies, and evaluation metrics accordingly.

Lastly, identifying the target audience is essential for crafting headlines that resonate with readers. Consideration should be given to demographic factors such as age, interests, and geographic location.

Understanding audience preferences and consumption habits aids in generating engaging and relevant content. Additionally, clarifying whether the AI robot will cater to a general audience or specific niche groups influences the tone, style, and language used in headline generation.

So, defining objectives means narrowing the news domains, specifying the robot's purpose, and identifying the target audience. This comprehensive understanding serves as a roadmap for subsequent steps, guiding the development process towards achieving the desired goals effectively.

Once you achieve this basic step, the next big step is data collection to build your bot. That is the topic for the next chapter.

CHAPTER TWO
DATA COLLECTION

Gather a diverse dataset of news articles relevant to the chosen topics. This dataset will be used to train the AI model.

Data collection for training an AI model to generate news headlines is a critical phase. This step lays the foundation for the system's performance and relevance. The process involves gathering a diverse and comprehensive dataset of news articles spanning various sources, topics, and viewpoints. Yes, you need a set. But firstly, it's essential to identify reputable sources known for their accuracy and credibility to ensure the quality of the data. This may include mainstream news outlets, specialized publications, blogs, and forums. Curating a diverse dataset ensures the model is exposed to a wide range of writing styles, tones, and perspectives, enhancing its ability to generate headlines that resonate with different audiences.

Furthermore, data collection entails scraping or accessing articles from online repositories, APIs, or databases. There are automated web scraping tools that can facilitate the extraction of large volumes of text efficiently. Care should be taken to respect copyright laws and terms of service when collecting data from external sources.

In addition to gathering text data, metadata such as publication dates, categories, and author information can provide valuable context for the training process. This metadata can be utilized to enrich the dataset and facilitate more nuanced learning by the AI model.

Further still, preprocessing steps like text cleaning, tokenization, and language normalization are often performed during data collection to standardize the format and improve the quality of the dataset. This ensures that the AI model receives clean and consistent input during training, leading to more accurate and reliable headline generation. We are going to talk more about that in the next chapter. In the meantime, you need to rest assured that making up a dataset is very crucial and fundamental to building your desired AI bot.

Yes, data collection for training an AI model has to do with gathering a diverse and extensive dataset of news articles from reputable sources, enriching it with metadata, and preprocessing the data to ensure quality and consistency. This meticulous process forms the backbone of the model's training and directly influences its performance in generating relevant and engaging news headlines.

Having said that, let us dwell a little bit on data cleaning in the next chapter.

CHAPTER THREE
PREPROCESSING

Preprocessing plays a crucial role in preparing the data for training an AI model to generate news headlines effectively. The process involves a series of steps aimed at cleaning, transforming, and standardizing the raw text data to enhance its quality and usability.

Begin data cleaning by removing irrelevant information, such as advertisements, HTML tags, and formatting artifacts, which could introduce noise and interfere with the learning process. This step helps narrow the dataset, making it more focused and conducive to effective training.

Secondly, text normalization techniques are applied to standardize the format and structure of the text data. This includes tasks such as converting text to lowercase, removing punctuation, and expanding contractions to ensure consistency across the dataset. Normalization helps reduce the dimensionality of the data and facilitates more efficient processing by the AI model.

Thirdly, tokenization is performed to break down the text into smaller units, such as words or subwords, which serve as the basic building blocks for the model's learning process. Tokenization enables the model to process and analyze the text at a more granular level, capturing subtle semantic nuances and patterns in the data.

Additionally, techniques such as stemming and lemmatization may be applied to reduce inflectional forms of words to their base or root forms, further improving the consistency and coherence of the dataset.

Moreover, handling missing or duplicate data, as well as addressing imbalances in the dataset, are important aspects of preprocessing that contribute to the overall quality and robustness of the AI model.

So, you can see that preprocessing involves a series of essential steps, including cleaning, normalization, tokenization, and data quality management. This in summary, is aimed at refining the raw text data and preparing it for effective training of the AI model. This meticulous process ensures that the model receives clean, consistent, and representative input, ultimately leading to more accurate and reliable headline generation. Otherwise, the AI gets confused, which may result in output that is outside your desired objectives.

It is now time to select your model. Let's see in the next chapter.

CHAPTER FOUR
MODEL SELECTION

Model selection is a pivotal step in the development of an AI system for generating news headlines, as it determines the architecture and capabilities of the underlying algorithm. Several factors must be considered when choosing a suitable model. This includes performance, scalability, interpretability, and computational efficiency.

One popular option for headline generation is the Generative Pre-trained Transformer (GPT) model, known for its ability to generate coherent and contextually relevant text based on input prompts. GPT leverages transformer architecture and large-scale pre-training on diverse text corpora, enabling it to capture complex linguistic patterns and generate human-like responses. Its flexibility and adaptability make it well-suited for a wide range of natural language processing tasks, including headline generation.

Alternatively, sequence-to-sequence (Seq2Seq) models offer another approach to headline generation by mapping input sequences to output sequences. These models consist of an encoder-decoder architecture, where the encoder processes the input text, and the decoder generates the corresponding headline. Seq2Seq models have been successfully applied to tasks such as machine translation and text summarization, making them a viable option for headline generation as well.

When selecting a model, considerations must also be given to factors such as computational resources, training data availability, and the specific requirements of the project. Additionally, pre-trained models like GPT may require fine-tuning on domain-specific data to optimize performance for headline generation tasks.

But what should be chosen of GPT and Seq2Seq models for a news site? No doubt you may wonder what would be my choice is I want to integrate on my own news site.

Both types of AI mentioned, namely natural language processing (NLP) models like GPT (Generative Pre-trained Transformer) and sequence-to-sequence models, have their own advantages and applications. However, in many cases, NLP models like GPT are often preferred over sequence-to-sequence models for tasks such as news headline generation. And I would ask you to opt for that.

NLP models like GPT have gained popularity due to their ability to generate human-like text based on input prompts. They excel at capturing complex linguistic patterns and context, making them well-suited for generating coherent and contextually relevant headlines. Additionally, pre-trained NLP models like GPT have been trained on vast amounts of text data, enabling them to leverage learned knowledge and generate diverse and high-quality headlines.

On the other hand, while sequence-to-sequence models are effective for tasks like machine translation and text summarization, they may not always perform as well for headline generation due to their inherent limitations in capturing context and generating fluent text.

All in all, selecting your model is one of the most

crucial phase of your project. It is the structure upon which everything rests. In addition, the preference for NLP models like GPT in news headline generation is driven by their superior performance in capturing semantic relationships, generating coherent text, and adapting to diverse writing styles and topics.

I have just shared my own preference. And trust me, that's actually what I would recommend for a news site. However, you are not bound by my recommendation. No.

The choice of model depends on the project's objectives, constraints, and performance metrics. Experimentation and evaluation of different models may be necessary to identify the most suitable option for you, for generating high-quality and engaging news headlines.

GET OR MAKE YOUR OWN MODEL

At this point, you are eager to have your own model. I think this is the simplest and most interesting of the whole project.

There are various platforms and frameworks that provide AI model resources. I will show you some of the most popular options. It is up to you if you if you would like to get a pre-trained model or opt DIY option. I will also include platforms that will give you tools to deploy and integrate your model into your site.

As I already said, below are some of the most popular platforms and tools to leverage for your personal model:

1. OpenAI's GPT (Generative Pre-trained Transformer): OpenAI offers access to its GPT models through APIs or pre-trained models that can be fine-tuned on your specific dataset. You can explore OpenAI's platform and documentation for more information on accessing and utilizing GPT for headline generation.

2. Hugging Face Transformers: Hugging Face provides a wide range of pre-trained transformer models,

including GPT variants, along with tools and libraries for fine-tuning and deploying these models. Their platform offers tutorials, documentation, and community support for training AI models for various natural language processing tasks, including headline generation.

3. Google Cloud AI Platform: Google Cloud offers AI Platform, which provides infrastructure and tools for training and deploying AI models at scale. You can leverage Google Cloud's services, such as TensorFlow and BERT (Bidirectional Encoder Representations from Transformers), for training chatbots tailored to your specific needs, including news headline generation.

4. Microsoft Azure AI: Microsoft Azure offers a suite of AI services and tools, including Azure Machine Learning, for developing and training custom AI models. You can explore Azure's services and documentation for resources and guidance on training chatbots for news headline generation.

5. DIY Approach: Alternatively, you can opt for a do-it-yourself approach by leveraging open-source libraries and frameworks such as TensorFlow, PyTorch, or Transformers. These frameworks provide building blocks and tools for training and fine-tuning AI models, allowing you to customize and tailor the chatbot according to your requirements.

When you have finally settled on your preferred model type, how do you proceed to train it. The next chapter is going to dwell a little bit on that.

CHAPTER FIVE
TRAINING

Training the selected model on the preprocessed dataset is a pivotal phase in the development of an AI system for generating news headlines. This is the time to expose the model to vast amounts of data and iteratively adjusting its parameters to minimize errors and improve performance. This process is called training.

Initially, the preprocessed dataset is divided into training, validation, and testing sets. The training set, comprising the majority of the data, is used to teach the model to recognize patterns and structures in news headlines. The validation set is utilized to fine-tune hyperparameters and monitor the model's performance during training, while the testing set evaluates the model's generalization and performance on unseen data.

During training, the model learns to generate headlines by adjusting its internal parameters based on feedback from the training data. This involves iteratively updating the model's weights through optimization algorithms such as stochastic gradient descent (SGD) or Adam. The objective is to minimize a loss function that quantifies the disparity between the model's predictions and the ground truth headlines in the training set.

The training process typically involves multiple epochs, where the entire dataset is passed through the model multiple times. As the training progresses, the model gradually improves its ability to generate coherent and relevant headlines by capturing intricate linguistic patterns and semantic relationships present in the data.

Furthermore, techniques such as regularization, dropout, and early stopping may be employed to prevent overfitting and enhance the model's generalization capabilities.

Overall, the training phase is a crucial stage in refining the AI model's ability to generate high-quality news headlines by learning from the patterns and structures inherent in the preprocessed dataset. This iterative process lays the groundwork for the model to produce accurate and engaging headlines that resonate with readers.

You are not done yet. There is a big need for further streamlining. And the next chapter will teach us how to do that.

CAPTER SIX
FINE-TUNING

I'm aware that you have already trained your model on a vast amount of general dataset. Fine-tuning the model is something else. You are going to adjust the model specifically for headline generation tasks. And it's a critical step aimed at optimizing its performance and enhancing its ability to generate accurate and engaging headlines. Fine-tuning involves moving the parameters of a pre-trained model, which has already been trained on a large general dataset, to better suit the characteristics of the headline generation task and the specific domain of news.

The fine-tuning process typically begins by initializing the model with weights learned during pre-training, such as those from a large-scale language model like GPT. These pre-trained models have already captured general linguistic patterns and semantics from vast amounts of text data, providing a strong foundation for further adaptation to specific tasks.

Next, the model is fine-tuned on a smaller, domain-specific dataset consisting of news headlines. This dataset may include examples of headlines from various sources, covering different topics and styles, ensuring the model learns to generate headlines that are relevant, informative, and engaging to readers.

During fine-tuning, the parameters of the model are adjusted through gradient descent optimization techniques, minimizing a loss function that quantifies the disparity between the model's predictions and the ground truth headlines in the training set. Hyperparameters such as learning rate, batch size, and regularization techniques are carefully tuned to optimize performance and prevent overfitting.

Additionally, techniques such as curriculum learning, where the model is gradually exposed to more challenging examples during training, and transfer learning, where knowledge learned from related tasks is leveraged to improve performance, may be employed to further enhance the fine-tuning process.

This step is essential for tailoring the model's capabilities to the specific requirements of the news domain, ultimately resulting in more accurate, relevant, and engaging headline generation. And trust me, this is your desire.

But how do you know the worth of your model. You have some evaluation work to do before you start enjoying it. Let's see how you do that in the next chapter.

CHAPTER SEVEN
EVALUATION

Evaluation is no less important step. You must assessing the quality of the generated headlines to ensure the effectiveness of the AI model for its intended purpose. What help do you have to do this? Well, various metrics are employed to measure different aspects of headline quality, including fluency, coherence, relevance, and novelty.

Let's take these one after the other.

Fluency refers to the linguistic quality of the generated headlines, assessing how grammatically correct and coherent they are. Metrics such as perplexity, which measures the uncertainty of the language model in predicting the next word, can be used to quantify fluency.

Coherence evaluates the logical flow and consistency of the generated headlines, assessing whether the ideas presented are logically connected and follow a coherent narrative structure. Techniques such as coherence modeling and coherence scoring algorithms can be utilized to measure coherence objectively.

Relevance assesses the extent to which the generated

headlines accurately reflect the content of the underlying news articles and address the intended topics. Evaluation methods may involve comparing the generated headlines to the corresponding ground truth headlines or leveraging external sources such as human annotators to assess relevance.

Novelty measures the originality and uniqueness of the generated headlines, assessing whether they offer new perspectives or insights compared to existing headlines. Novelty metrics may involve comparing the generated headlines to a reference corpus of headlines to identify overlaps and redundancies.

Additionally, subjective evaluation methods such as human judgment and user feedback can provide valuable insights into the perceived quality and effectiveness of the generated headlines. Human evaluators can assess aspects such as readability, informativeness, and engagement, providing qualitative feedback that complements quantitative metrics.

In essence, evaluation is a multifaceted process that involves assessing various dimensions of headline quality using a combination of objective metrics and subjective judgment. By systematically evaluating the generated headlines, developers can identify strengths and weaknesses in the AI model and iteratively improve its performance to better meet the needs and expectations of yours.

I assume that at this point, you have done all you are supposed to do to come up with a high quality model for your news website. The next question is how will you introduce your model into your site? Let me show you in the next chapter.

CHAPTER EIGHT
DEPLOYMENT

Deployment marks the transition from development to practical implementation, where the trained model is integrated into a system capable of generating headlines in real-time in response to input prompts. This process involves several key steps to ensure the seamless and efficient operation of the AI system.

Firstly, the trained model is encapsulated or wrapped within a software framework or application programming interface (API) to facilitate its integration into the deployment environment. This may involve packaging the model along with any necessary dependencies and infrastructure components into a deployable unit, such as a Docker container or a serverless function.

Next, you provisioned and configured the deployment infrastructure to support the real-time execution of the model. Among the things you need to do is setting up scalable computing resources, such as cloud-based virtual machines or container orchestration platforms. This is what will handle varying workloads and your demand.

Once the deployment infrastructure is in place, you

deployed the model and exposed it through an API endpoint, allowing external systems or applications to interact with it programmatically. This is what will enables you to submit input prompts, such as text snippets or keywords, and receive corresponding headlines generated by the model in response.

Furthermore, implement monitoring and logging mechanisms to track the performance and usage of the deployed model in real-time. This includes monitoring resource utilization, latency, error rates, and throughput to ensure the system meets service level objectives and your expectations.

Finally, ongoing maintenance and support processes are established to address issues, apply updates, and optimize performance as needed. This may involve periodic retraining of the model with fresh data to adapt to evolving trends and preferences in news content.

In this chapter, we said that deployment involves integrating the trained model into a real-time system, provisioning scalable infrastructure, socializing it through an API endpoint, and establishing monitoring and maintenance processes to ensure its reliable and efficient operation. This enables you to access the AI-powered headline generation capabilities seamlessly, facilitating the dissemination of timely and relevant news content.

In a latter chapter, I'm going to talk a little bit about the model's maintenance. In the meantime, let's look at testing and optimization in the next chapter.

CHAPTER NINE
TESTING AND OPTIMIZATION

Once the model is deployed, testing and optimization are critical phases in the development for generating news headlines, ensuring its reliability, accuracy, and effectiveness in real-world scenarios. This process involves a series of systematic evaluations and iterative improvements to identify and address issues, biases, and performance bottlenecks.

Firstly, you employ various testing methodologies to assess the model's performance across different dimensions, including functionality, accuracy, robustness, and scalability. You need to conduct unit tests, integration tests, and end-to-end tests to validate the model's behavior under diverse conditions and input scenarios. This will help identify bugs, inconsistencies, and edge cases that may affect the quality of the generated headlines.

Moreover, you will need to utilize evaluation metrics such as fluency, coherence, relevance, and novelty to quantify the quality of the model's output and compare it against desired benchmarks. These metrics provide actionable insights into areas for improvement and guide optimization efforts.

Furthermore, you will need to apply optimization techniques to enhance the efficiency and accuracy of the model. This may involve fine-tuning hyperparameters, adjusting model architecture, optimizing inference algorithms, and incorporating domain-specific knowledge to improve performance. Techniques such as pruning, quantization, and model distillation may also be employed to reduce model size and computational complexity without compromising accuracy.

Additionally, you will need to implement bias detection and mitigation strategies to address potential biases in the model's output, such as gender, racial, or ideological biases. This may involve analyzing the distribution of generated headlines across different demographic groups, identifying biases, and implementing corrective measures to promote fairness and inclusivity.

Overall, testing and optimization are iterative processes that involve continuous refinement of the AI model to ensure its reliability, accuracy, and fairness in generating news headlines. By systematically evaluating the model's performance and addressing any identified issues or biases, you can enhance its effectiveness and usability in real-world applications.

CHAPTER TEN
MONITORING AND MAINTENANCE

Monitoring and maintenance are very important practices to uphold the performance, reliability, and relevance of the AI model for generating news headlines over time. Continuous oversight and proactive interventions help forestall issues, adapt to changing circumstances, and ensure sustained effectiveness in delivering high-quality headlines.

Firstly, performance metrics and key performance indicators (KPIs) should be established to measure the AI model's performance and effectiveness in generating headlines. These metrics may include accuracy, fluency, coherence, relevance, engagement, and your satisfaction. Regular monitoring of these metrics enables early detection of deviations or deterioration in performance, prompting timely interventions.

Furthermore, monitoring encompasses tracking the model's resource utilization, latency, throughput, and error rates to ensure optimal operational efficiency and scalability. This involves leveraging monitoring tools and dashboards to visualize performance metrics in real-time and set up alerts for abnormal behavior or performance degradation.

Periodic maintenance involves updating the model with new data to keep it up-to-date with evolving trends, topics, and your preferences. This may involve retraining the model periodically on fresh datasets to adapt to changes in the news landscape and ensure its relevance and accuracy over time. Additionally, fine-tuning hyperparameters and optimizing model architecture may be necessary to address performance bottlenecks or improve efficiency.

Moreover, continuous evaluation of the model's output for biases, errors, or inconsistencies is crucial to maintain fairness, diversity, and inclusivity in the generated headlines. Bias detection mechanisms and fairness audits can help identify and mitigate biases in the model's output, ensuring equitable representation and treatment of diverse perspectives.

In summary, monitoring and maintenance involve ongoing oversight, evaluation, and adaptation of the AI model to uphold its performance, relevance, and fairness in generating news headlines. By proactively addressing issues, updating with new data, and making necessary adjustments, you can ensure the continued effectiveness and reliability of the AI model over time.

CHAPTER ELEVEN
ETHICAL CONSIDERATIONS

The value of ethical considerations cannot be overemphasized. They are paramount in the development and deployment of AI systems for generating news headlines, given their potential impact on public discourse, societal perceptions, and individual privacy. Addressing ethical implications such as bias, misinformation, and privacy concerns requires a comprehensive approach that prioritizes transparency, accountability, and fairness throughout the AI lifecycle.

One critical aspect of ethical considerations is mitigating biases in the AI model's output, which may stem from biases present in the training data or inherent in the model architecture. Techniques such as bias detection, fairness testing, and algorithmic audits can help identify and address biases in the model's predictions, ensuring equitable representation and treatment of diverse perspectives.

Moreover, combating misinformation and disinformation is essential to uphold the integrity and credibility of news content generated by AI systems. Fact-checking mechanisms, source verification, and credibility scoring algorithms can help verify the accuracy and reliability of news articles before generating headlines, reducing the dissemination of false or misleading information.

Privacy concerns arise from the potential collection and processing of sensitive personal data, such as your interactions and preferences, in the course of generating personalized news headlines. Implementing privacy-preserving measures such as data anonymization, consent management, and robust security protocols can help safeguard user privacy and prevent unauthorized access or misuse of personal information.

Furthermore, promoting transparency and accountability in AI systems involves personally understanding the underlying algorithms, data sources, and decision-making processes and exposing such to stakeholders and users. This fosters trust, enables informed decision-making, and empowers users to understand and scrutinize the implications of AI-generated news headlines.

What we have said in this chapter in conclusion, ethical considerations in AI-driven news headline generation require proactive measures to address biases, misinformation, and privacy concerns, fostering transparency, accountability, and fairness in the development and deployment of AI systems. By integrating ethical principles into the design and operation of these systems, you can reduce risks and uphold ethical standards in the dissemination of news content.

CONCLUSION

By meticulously following the outlined steps, you can successfully develop an AI robot equipped to research and generate news headlines for your blog or website. Each step, from defining objectives to addressing ethical considerations, contributes to the creation of a robust and effective system. By defining clear objectives, gathering diverse datasets, selecting suitable models, and training and fine-tuning them specifically for headline generation tasks, you lay a solid foundation for success.

Moreover, continuous evaluation, monitoring, and maintenance ensure that the AI robot remains effective and relevant over time. Regular updates, incorporating new data and advancements in AI technology, help keep the system adaptive and responsive to evolving trends and user needs. Additionally, ongoing efforts to mitigate biases, combat misinformation, and uphold ethical standards contribute to the system's credibility and trustworthiness.

However, the journey doesn't end with the creation of the AI robot. It's crucial to stay informed about the latest advancements in AI and remain vigilant to emerging ethical considerations and societal implications. By staying abreast of developments in the field, you can leverage new techniques, methodologies, and tools to enhance the performance and capabilities of your system.

All in all, while the process of creating an AI robot for news headline generation may be complex and multifaceted, following these steps diligently can lead to the development of a powerful and impactful tool for delivering timely and relevant news content. By embracing continuous learning and adaptation, you can ensure that your system remains at the forefront of innovation, delivering value to you and contributing positively to the evolving media world.

ABOUT THE AUTHOR

Thanks for reading our book. For questions, reach out to the author on the email address provided above, on the title page.

If you like the book, kindly gave us a minute more or two, rate the work or tell others what you feel about your exploration of the work.

Thanks once again — I. O. FAITH

www.ingramcontent.com/pod-product-compliance
Lightning Source LLC
Chambersburg PA
CBHW070956220526
45471CB00007B/3052